Aler

Merry Christmas

Dear Nick
Dear Nick
1996 —

Maybe one day we'll
be reading your
poems!!

BOOKS BY LOUISE GLÜCK

The House on Marshland

# The
# House
## on
# Marshland

## LOUISE GLÜCK

## The Ecco Press

Copyright © 1971, 1972, 1973, 1974, 1975 by Louise Glück
First published in 1975 by The Ecco Press
100 West Broad Street, Hopewell, NJ 08525
Published simultaneously in Canada by
Penguin Books Canada Ltd., Ontario

Library of Congress Cataloging in Publication Data

Glück, Louise, 1943–
    The house on marshland.

    (The American poetry series; v. 5)
    Poems.
    I.  Title
PS3557.L8H6        811'.5'4        74-21764
ISBN 0-88001-294-3

Printed in U.S.A.
DESIGNED BY LORETTA LI

Sixth Printing, 1992

ACKNOWLEDGMENTS

*American Poetry Review:*    "Brennende Liebe"
        "The School Children"
        "Still Life"
        "Japonica"
        "The Apple Trees"

*Antaeus:*    "The Swimmer"
        "Here Are My Black Clothes"
        "The Fire"
        "Messengers"

*Equal Time:*    "Jeanne d'Arc"
        "Love Poem"

*The Goddard Journal:*    "Abishag"

*Gulf Stream:*    "12. 6. 71"

*The Iowa Review:*    "The Pond"
        "For My Mother"
        "Gemini"

*Lillabulero:*    "Poem"
        "For Jane Myers"

*The Nation:*    "Departure"
        "The Letters"

*New American Review:*    "Gretel in Darkness"

*The New Yorker:*    "All Hallows"

*Poetry:*    "The Undertaking"
        "The Magi"
        "Archipelago"
        "The Shad-blow Tree"
        "The Fortress"

*Salmagundi:*    "Pomegranate"

*With love and gratitude*

KAREN  KENNERLY

TOM  GILSON

ELLEN  BRYANT  VOIGT

I would like to thank the
National Endowment for the Arts
for its support.

# Contents

# Contents

ALL HALLOWS

# All Hallows

Even now this landscape is assembling.
The hills darken. The oxen
sleep in their blue yoke,
the fields having been
picked clean, the sheaves
bound evenly and piled at the roadside
among cinquefoil, as the toothed moon rises:

This is the barrenness
of harvest or pestilence.
And the wife leaning out the window
with her hand extended, as in payment,
and the seeds
distinct, gold, calling
*Come here*
*Come here, little one*

And the soul creeps out of the tree.

# The Pond

Night covers the pond with its wing.
Under the ringed moon I can make out
your face swimming among minnows and the small
echoing stars. In the night air
the surface of the pond is metal.

Within, your eyes are open. They contain
a memory I recognize, as though
we had been children together. Our ponies
grazed on the hill, they were gray
with white markings. Now they graze
with the dead who wait
like children under their granite breastplates,
lucid and helpless:

The hills are far away. They rise up
blacker than childhood.
What do you think of, lying so quietly
by the water? When you look that way I want
to touch you, but do not, seeing
as in another life we were of the same blood.

# Gretel in Darkness

This is the world we wanted.
All who would have seen us dead
are dead. I hear the witch's cry
break in the moonlight through a sheet
of sugar: God rewards.
Her tongue shrivels into gas. . . .

         Now, far from women's arms
and memory of women, in our father's hut
we sleep, are never hungry.
Why do I not forget?
My father bars the door, bars harm
from this house, and it is years.

No one remembers. Even you, my brother,
summer afternoons you look at me as though
you meant to leave,
as though it never happened.
But I killed for you. I see armed firs,
the spires of that gleaming kiln—

Nights I turn to you to hold me
but you are not there.
Am I alone? Spies
hiss in the stillness, Hansel,
we are there still and it is real, real,
that black forest and the fire in earnest.

# For My Mother

It was better when we were
together in one body.
Thirty years. Screened
through the green glass
of your eye, moonlight
filtered into my bones
as we lay
in the big bed, in the dark,
waiting for my father.
Thirty years. He closed
your eyelids with
two kisses. And then spring
came and withdrew from me
the absolute
knowledge of the unborn,
leaving the brick stoop
where you stand, shading
your eyes, but it is
night, the moon
is stationed in the beech tree,
round and white among
the small tin markers of the stars:
Thirty years. A marsh
grows up around the house.
Schools of spores circulate
behind the shades, drift through
gauze flutterings of vegetation.

# Archipelago

The tenth year we came upon immense sunlight, a relief
of islands locked into the water. These became our course.
Eleven months we drifted, toward the twelfth
wandered into docile ocean, a harbor. We prepared for
                                                    peace.

Weeks passed. And then the captain saw
the mouth closing that defined our port—we are
devoured. Other voices stir. Water
sneers against our ship, our shrunk number runs
in two packs: madness and suicide. The twelfth year
the captain calls his name, it has no meaning, and the crew
shrieks in its extremity.

# The Magi

Toward world's end, through the bare
beginnings of winter, they are traveling again.
How many winters have we seen it happen,
watched the same sign come forward as they pass
cities sprung around this route their gold
engraved on the desert, and yet
held our peace, these
being the Wise, come to see at the accustomed hour
nothing changed: roofs, the barn
blazing in darkness, all they wish to see.

# The Shad-blow Tree

*—for Tom*

## 1 THE TREE

It is all here,
luminous water, the imprinted sapling
matched, branch by branch,
to the lengthened
tree in the lens, as it was
against the green, poisoned landscape.

## 2 THE LATENT IMAGE

One year he focused on a tree
until, through sunlight pure as never afterward, he saw
the season, early spring, work upon those limbs
its white flower, which the eye
retains: deep in the brain
the shad-blow coins its leaf in this context,
among monuments, continuous with such frozen forms
as have become the trained vine,
root, rock, and all things perishing.

# Messengers

You have only to wait, they will find you.
The geese flying low over the marsh,
glittering in black water.
They find you.

And the deer—
how beautiful they are,
as though their bodies did not impede them.
Slowly they drift into the open
through bronze panels of sunlight.

Why would they stand so still
if they were not waiting?
Almost motionless, until their cages rust,
the shrubs shiver in the wind,
squat and leafless.

You have only to let it happen:
that cry—*release, release*—like the moon
wrenched out of earth and rising
full in its circle of arrows

until they come before you
like dead things, saddled with flesh,
and you above them, wounded and dominant.

# The Murderess

You call me sane, insane—I tell you men
were leering to themselves; she saw.
She was my daughter. She would pare
her skirt until her thighs grew
longer, till the split tongue slid into her brain.
He had her smell. Fear
will check beauty, but she had no fear. She talked
doubletalk, she lent
her heat to Hell's: Commissioner, the sun
opens to consume the Virgin on the fifteenth day.
It was like slitting fish. And then the stain
dissolved, and God presided at her body.

# Flowering Plum

In spring from the black branches of the flowering plum tree
the woodthrush issues its routine
message of survival. Where does such happiness come from
as the neighbors' daughter reads into that singing,
and matches? All afternoon she sits
in the partial shade of the plum tree, as the mild wind
floods her immaculate lap with blossoms, greenish white
and white, leaving no mark, unlike
the fruit that will inscribe
unraveling dark stains in heavier winds, in summer.

# Nativity Poem

It is the evening
of the birth of god.
Singing &
with gold instruments
the angels bear down
upon the barn, their wings
neither white
wax nor marble. So
they have been recorded:
burnished,
literal in the composed air,
they raise their harps above
the beasts likewise gathering,
the lambs & all the startled
silken chickens. . . . And Joseph,
off to one side, has touched
his cheek, meaning
he is weeping—

But how small he is, withdrawn
from the hollow of his mother's life,
the raw flesh bound
in linen as the stars yield
light to delight his sense
for whom there is no ornament.

# To Autumn

*—for Keith Althaus*

Morning quivers in the thorns; above the budded snowdrops
caked with dew like little virgins, the azalea bush
ejects its first leaves, and it is spring again.
The willow waits its turn, the coast
is coated with a faint green fuzz, anticipating
mold. Only I
do not collaborate, having
flowered earlier. I am no longer young. What
of it? Summer approaches, and the long
decaying days of autumn when I shall begin
the great poems of my middle period.

# Still Life

Father has his arm around Tereze.
She squints. My thumb
is in my mouth: my fifth autumn.
Near the copper beech
the spaniel dozes in shadows.
Not one of us does not avert his eyes.

Across the lawn, in full sun, my mother
stands behind her camera.

# For Jane Myers

Sap rises from the sodden ditch
and glues two green ears to the dead
birch twig. Perilous beauty—
and already Jane is digging out
her colored tennis shoes,
one mauve, one yellow, like large crocuses.

And by the laundromat
the Bartletts in their tidy yard—

as though it were not
wearying, wearying

to hear in the bushes
the mild harping of the breeze,
the daffodils flocking and honking—

Look how the bluet falls apart, mud
pockets the seed.
Months, years, then the dull blade of the wind.
It is spring! We are going to die!

And now April raises up her plaque of flowers
and the heart
expands to admit its adversary.

# Gratitude

Do not think I am not grateful for your small
kindness to me.
I like small kindnesses.
In fact I actually prefer them to the more
substantial kindness, that is always eying you,
like a large animal on a rug,
until your whole life reduces
to nothing but waking up morning after morning
cramped, and the bright sun shining on its tusks.

# Poem

In the early evening, as now, a man is bending
over his writing table.
Slowly he lifts his head; a woman
appears, carrying roses.
Her face floats to the surface of the mirror,
marked with the green spokes of rose stems.

It is a form
of suffering: then always the transparent page
raised to the window until its veins emerge
as words finally filled with ink.

And I am meant to understand
what binds them together
or to the gray house held firmly in place by dusk

because I must enter their lives:
it is spring, the pear tree
filming with weak, white blossoms.

# The School Children

The children go forward with their little satchels.
And all morning the mothers have labored
to gather the late apples, red and gold,
like words of another language.

And on the other shore
are those who wait behind great desks
to receive these offerings.

How orderly they are—the nails
on which the children hang
their overcoats of blue or yellow wool.

And the teachers shall instruct them in silence
and the mothers shall scour the orchards for a way out,
drawing to themselves the gray limbs of the fruit trees
bearing so little ammunition.

# Jeanne d'Arc

It was in the fields. The trees grew still,
a light passed through the leaves speaking
of Christ's great grace: I heard.
My body hardened into armor.

                        Since the guards
gave me over to darkness I have prayed to God
and now the voices answer I must be
transformed to fire, for God's purpose,
and have bid me kneel
to bless my King, and thank
the enemy to whom I owe my life.

# Departure

My father is standing on a railroad platform.
Tears pool in his eyes, as though the face
glimmering in the window were the face of someone
he was once. But the other has forgotten;
as my father watches, he turns away,
drawing the shade over his face,
goes back to his reading.

And already in its deep groove
the train is waiting with its breath of ashes.

# Gemini

There is a soul in me
It is asking
to be given its body

It is asking
to be given blue eyes
a skull matted

with black hair
that shape
already formed & detaching

So the past put forth
a house filled with
asters & white lilac

a child
in her cotton dress
the lawn, the copper beech—

such of my own lives
I have cast off—the sunlight
chipping at the curtains

& the wicker chairs
uncovered, winter after winter,
as the stars finally

thicken & descend as snow

# THE APPLE TREES

# The Undertaking

The darkness lifts, imagine, in your lifetime.
There you are—cased in clean bark you drift
through weaving rushes, fields flooded with cotton.
You are free. The river films with lilies,
shrubs appear, shoots thicken into palm. And now
all fear gives way: the light
looks after you, you feel the waves' goodwill
as arms widen over the water; Love,

the key is turned. Extend yourself—
it is the Nile, the sun is shining,
everywhere you turn is luck.

# Pomegranate

First he gave me
his heart. It was
red fruit containing
many seeds, the skin
leathery, unlikely.
I preferred
to starve, bearing
out my training.
Then he said Behold
how the world looks, minding
your mother. I
peered under his arm:
What had she done
with color & odor?
Whereupon he said Now *there*
is a woman who loves
with a vengeance, adding
Consider she is in her element:
the trees turning to her, whole
villages going under
although in hell
the bushes are still
burning with pomegranates.
At which
he cut one open & began
to suck. When he looked up at last
it was to say My dear
you are your own
woman, finally, but examine
this grief your mother
parades over our heads
remembering
that she is one to whom
these depths were not offered.

# Brennende Liebe

*—1904*

Dearest love: The roses are in bloom again,
cream and rose, to either side of the brick walk.
I pass among them with my white umbrella
as the sun beats down upon the oval plots like pools
in the grass, willows and the grove
of statuary. So the days go by. Fine days
I take my tea beneath the elm
half turned, as though you were beside me saying
*Flowers that could take your breath away. . . .*
And always on the tray
a rose, and always the sun branded on the river
and the men in summer suits, in linen, and the girls,
their skirts circled in shadow. . . . Last night
I dreamed that you did not return.
Today is fair. The little maid filled a silver bowl
shaped like a swan with roses for my bedside,
with the dark red they call *Brennende Liebe*,
which I find so beautiful.

# Abishag

## 1

At God's word David's kinsmen cast
through Canaan:
It was understood
the king was dying
as they said
outright
so that my father turned to me saying
*How much have I ever asked of you*
to which I answered
*Nothing*
as I remembered

So the sun rose from his shoulders:
blue air, the desert, the small
yellowing village

When I see myself
it is still as I was then,
beside the well, staring
into the hollowed gourd half filled
with water, where the dark braid
grazing the left shoulder was recorded
though the face
was featureless
of which they did not say
*She has the look of one who seeks*
*some greater and destroying passion*:

They took me as I was.
Not one among the kinsmen touched me,
not one among the slaves.
No one will touch me now.

2

In the recurring dream my father
stands at the doorway in his black cassock
telling me to choose
among my suitors, each of whom
will speak my name once
until I lift my hand in signal.
On my father's arm I listen
for not three sounds: *Abishag,*
but two: *my love—*

I tell you if it is my own will
binding me I cannot be saved.
And yet in the dream, in the half-light
of the stone house, they looked
so much alike. Sometimes I think
the voices were themselves
identical, and that I raised my hand
chiefly in weariness. I hear my father saying
*Choose, choose.* But they were not alike
and to select death, O yes I can
believe that of my body.

# 12. 6. 71

You having turned from me
I dreamed we were
beside a pond between two mountains
It was night
The moon throbbed in its socket
Where the spruces thinned
three deer wakened & broke cover
and I heard my name
not spoken but cried out
so that I reached for you
except the sheet was ice
as they had come for me
who, one by one, were likewise
introduced to darkness
And the snow
which has not ceased since
began

# Love Poem

There is always something to be made of pain.
Your mother knits.
She turns out scarves in every shade of red.
They were for Christmas, and they kept you warm
while she married over and over, taking you
along. How could it work,
when all those years she stored her widowed heart
as though the dead come back.
No wonder you are the way you are,
afraid of blood, your women
like one brick wall after another.

# Northwood Path

For my part
we are as we were
on the path
that afternoon:
it is
October, I can see
the sun sink
drawing out
our parallel
shadows. And you,
for example what
were you thinking, so
attentive to your
shoes? I recall
we spoke of
your car
the whole length
of the woods:
in so much withering
the pokeweed had
branched into its
purplish berry—so
desire called
love into being.
But always the choice
was on both sides
characteristic,
as you said,
in the dark you came
to need,
you would do it again

# he Fire

Had you died when we were together
I would have wanted nothing of you.
Now I think of you as dead, it is better.

Often, in the cool early evenings of the spring
when, with the first leaves,
all that is deadly enters the world,
I build a fire for us of pine and apple wood;
repeatedly
the flames flare and diminish
as the night comes on in which
we see one another so clearly—

And in the days we are contented
as formerly
in the long grass,
in the woods' green doors and shadows.

And you never say
*Leave me*
since the dead do not like being alone.

# The Fortress

There is nothing now. To learn
the lesson past disease
was easier. In God's hotel I saw
my name and number stapled to a vein
as Marcy funneled its corrective air
toward Placid. I can breathe
again. I watch the mountain under siege
by ice give way to blocks of dungeons,
ovens manned by wives. I understand.
They coil their hair, they turn their
music on as, humming to herself, the night-
nurse smoothes her uniform. This is
the proper pain. The lights are out. Love
forms in the human body.

# The Swimmer

You sat in the tub.
No sand stirred, the dead
waited in the ocean.
Then the tapwater
flooded over you,
sapphire and emerald.

The beach
is as you found it,
littered with objects.
They have brought me here;
I rifle through them,
shell and bone, and am not satisfied.

What brought me to rest was your body.
Far away you turn your head:
through still grass the wind
moves into a human language

and the darkness comes,
the long nights
pass into stationary darkness.

Only the sea moves.
It takes on color, onyx and manganese.
If you are there it will release you
as when, among the tame waves,
I saw your worn face,
your long arms making for shore—

The waves come forward,
we are traveling together.

# The Letters

It is night for the last time.
For the last time your hands
gather on my body.

Tomorrow it will be autumn.
We will sit together on the balcony
watching the dry leaves drift over the village
like the letters we will burn,
one by one, in our separate houses.

Such a quiet night.
Only your voice murmuring
*You're wet, you want to*
and the child
sleeps as though he were not born.

In the morning it will be autumn.
We will walk together in the small garden
among stone benches and the shrubs
still sheeted in mist
like furniture left for a long time.

Look how the leaves drift in the darkness.
We have burned away
all that was written on them.

# aponica

The trees are flowering
on the hill.
They are bearing
large solitary blossoms,
japonica,
as when you came to me
mistakenly
carrying such flowers
having snapped them
from the thin branches.
The rain had stopped. Sunlight
motioned through the leaves.
But death
also has its flower,
it is called
contagion, it is
red or white, the color
of japonica—
You stood there,
your hands full of flowers.
How could I not take them
since they were a gift?

# The Apple Trees

Your son presses against me
his small intelligent body.

I stand beside his crib
as in another dream
you stood among trees hung
with bitten apples
holding out your arms.
I did not move
but saw the air dividing
into panes of color—at the very last
I raised him to the window saying
*See what you have made*
and counted out the whittled ribs,
the heart on its blue stalk
as from among the trees
the darkness issued:

In the dark room your son sleeps.
The walls are green, the walls
are spruce and silence.
I wait to see how he will leave me.
Already on his hand the map appears
as though you carved it there,
the dead fields, women rooted to the river.

LOUISE GLÜCK lives in Vermont with her husband and son. She teaches at Williams College. Her recent collection of poetry *Triumph of Achilles* received the National Book Critics Circle Award for Poetry, the Boston Globe Literary Press Award for Poetry, and the Poetry Society of America's Melville Kane Award.